CW00481283

CONTENTS

RECIPES INDEX 116

INTRODUCTION

A blender is an electric mixing machine used during food preparation to liquidize, chop or puree food. A blender works best with soft foods, and can make juices and smoothies. Some blenders are however powerful enough to handle harder tasks meant for food processors.

Uses of a blender

A blender is a versatile kitchen equipment which can perform various tasks including;

- Blending; instant puddings,
- Blending cream pie fillings,
- Blending custards,
- Blending frozen concentrated juices,
- Blending batter for pancakes,
- Blending ice cream shakes,
- Pureeing soft or cooked foods,
- Making eggnog,
- Making bread /cookie/cracker crumbs
- Making salad dressings

There are various types of blenders, all with different capabilities and all designed to make various kitchen tasks easier for you.

Types of blenders

Immersion Blenders

These are also known as hand or stick blenders. They have a long stick-like look, with blades at the bottom. They are easy to use; simply immerse the blender in your container holding food and the blades do the blending. These blenders are compact making them ideal for smaller kitchens. Because these blenders are not as high powered as the countertop blenders, they are more suitable for simpler blending tasks of soft ingredients. Immersion blenders are mostly cordless making them portable.

Single-serve Blenders

These are also known as personal blenders. They are easy to use. With these types of blenders, you can drink from the same jar you use to blend. Most single-serve blenders also come with a lid for the jar to double it as a smoothie cup so you can enjoy your drinks on the move.

Smoothie Blenders

These blenders are high powered and mostly come with a number of speed settings to give you precise control over your blending. Smoothie blenders can crush ice and others come with different size jars to suit your serving needs.

Power Food Blenders

These blenders are just like smoothie blenders only with more capabilities. They also have many different attachments and features. They not only make great smoothies and milkshakes, but also have features for chopping, grinding, mincing, pureeing, dicing, and more.

Professional Blenders

These types of blenders are commercial hence they are made from top notch materials and have very powerful motors to enable them carry out hard commercial blending tasks easily and precisely.

These types have the ability to blend all types of ingredients quickly and perfectly. Other than blending, these blenders are also able to chop, grind, puree and even cook! They are easy to clean and maintain as they use an advanced self-cleaning technology.

Professional blenders are very expensive and usually have warranties of up to 7 years.

Factors to consider when shopping for a blender

When getting a blender, consider getting one that is;

- **Multi-purpose** – the more a blender can perform the better,
- **Easy to use and clean**
- **The right size for you** – check your available space,
- **Affordable** – get one that gives you value for your money,
- **Has warranty** – in case it malfunctions and you need to take it back.

As you can see, various blender types perform different tasks and are suitable for different situations. Depending on your need, there is definitely a blender type for you.

NINJA ULTIMA BLENDER

Mental Beet Booster

Servings:2
Cooking Time:x

Ingredients:
- 2 beets, peeled and quartered,
- 2 pink grapefruits, peeled and quartered,
- 10 basil leaves,
- 3 tablespoons agave or honey,
- 1 1/2 cups water,
- 1 cup ice cubes

Directions:
1. Place the Top Blades in the Pitcher and add all of the ingredients in the order listed.*
2. Select Speed 1 and flip the switch to START. Slowly increase to Speed 6 and blend until smooth.

Apple Almond Power Smoothie

Servings:1
Cooking Time:x

Ingredients:

- 1 apple, peeled, cut in half,
- 1 banana, peeled, cut in half,
- 1 tablespoon almond butter,
- 1 scoop protein powder,
- 1 cup almond milk,
- 5 to 6 ice cubes

Directions:

1. Place all of the ingredients into the Nutri Ninja
2. cup in the order listed. PULSE until smooth. Remove the blades from the cup after blending.
3. Go ahead, embrace your inner meal prepper. We hear you, making smoothies the night before is a huge time saver. But, heads up, never store your smoothies with the blade assembly attached—active ingredients in some foods may lead to pressure buildup and possible injury. Store them with Sip & Seal Lids instead.

Farfalle With Sundried Tomato Sauce

Servings:4
Cooking Time:x

Ingredients:

- 1 28-ounce can whole tomatoes, with juices,
- 6 ounces sun-dried tomatoes packed in olive oil,
- 1 onion, chopped,
- 4 cloves garlic, chopped,
- 1/2 cup dry red wine,
- 1/2 teaspoon red pepper flakes,
- 1 tablespoon olive oil,
- 1 pound ground turkey,
- Kosher salt and pepper,
- 1/4 bunch basil, chopped,
- 2 tablespoons reserved for garnish,
- 4 cups farfalle, cooked,
- Parmesan cheese, grated as garnish

Directions:

1. Place tomatoes with juice, sun-dried tomatoes, red wine and red pepper flakes into the 72 ounce Pitcher fitted with the Bottom Blades only. Secure the lid.
2. Select Speed 1 and flip the switch to START. Process until chunky smooth.
3. Heat oil over medium heat and sauté onion and garlic until softened. Add ground turkey and cook while breaking up with the back of a spoon until done.
4. Stir in tomato sauce from blender, basil, salt and pepper and bring to a boil. Reduce heat and simmer until thickened, about 20 minutes.
5. Serve sauce ladled over pasta, garnished with basil and cheese.

Edamame Sesame Hummus

Servings:6-8
Cooking Time:x

Ingredients:

- 3 cups frozen shelled edamame, cooked, until tender,
- 2 cloves garlic, peeled,
- 1/2 cup water, plus more if needed,
- 1/4 cup lemon juice,
- 1/4 cup olive oil,
- 1/2 teaspoon ground cumin, salt and pepper to taste,
- black sesame seeds, as garnish

Directions:

1. Using the Bottom Blades in the Pitcher, add all of the ingredients, except sesame seeds.
2. Select Speed 1 and flip the switch to START. Slowly increase to Speed 3 and blend until smooth.
3. Add additional liquid if a thinner consistency is desired.
4. Garnish with black sesame seeds.

Ginger Pear Defense

Servings:2-3
Cooking Time:x

Ingredients:

- 3 pears, cored,
- 1/4 cantaloupe, peeled,
- 1 lemon, peeled,
- 1-inch fresh ginger, peeled,
- 2 cups ice cubes

Directions:

1. Place the Top Blades in the Pitcher and add all of the ingredients in the order listed.*
2. Select Speed 1 and flip the switch to START. Slowly increase to Speed 8 and blend until smooth.
3. Go ahead, embrace your inner meal prepper. We hear you, making smoothies the night before is a huge time saver. But, heads up, never store your smoothies with the blade assembly attached—active ingredients in some foods may lead to pressure buildup and possible injury. Store them with Sip & Seal Lids instead.

Breakfast Sausage Patties

Servings:x
Cooking Time:x

Ingredients:

- 1/2 pound chicken thighs, cleaned and well-chilled
- 1/2 pound boneless pork chops, quartered and well-chilled
- 1 small apple, peeled, cored and chopped
- 1 teaspoon dried thyme
- 1/4 teaspoon ground nutmeg
- salt and pepper to taste

Directions:

1. Place the Top Blades in the Pitcher and add all of the ingredients. PULSE to a fine chop consistency. Do not overprocess.
2. Remove mixture from the Pitcher and form into 6 patties. Place patties on a foil-lined rimmed baking sheet and broil on high 5 inches from the heating element.
3. Turn once while broiling. When done, the patties will be browned and the centers fully cooked, about 6 minutes per side.
4. Serve hot.

Old Fashioned Chocolate Mint Shake

Servings:2-3
Cooking Time:x

Ingredients:

- 2 cups mint chip nondairy frozen dessert,
- 1/4 cup dairy-free chocolate syrup,
- 1 cup vanilla soy milk,
- 1 1/2 cups ice cubes

Directions:

1. Place the Top Blades in the Pitcher and add all of the ingredients in the order listed.
2. Select Speed 3 and flip the switch to START. Slowly increase to Speed 8 and blend until smooth.
3. Divide among glasses and serve.

Melon Immune Booster

Servings:1 14-ounce Serving
Cooking Time:x

Ingredients:
- 1/4 orange, peeled
- 1/2 cup frozen mango chunks
- 1/2 cup cantaloupe
- 1 cup almond milk
- 1/2 teaspoon honey

Directions:
1. Place all ingredients into the Ninja Ultima Single Serve in the order listed. PULSE until smooth. Remove the blades from the cup after blending.
2. Go ahead, embrace your inner meal prepper. We hear you, making smoothies the night before is a huge time saver. But, heads up, never store your smoothies with the blade assembly attached—active ingredients in some foods may lead to pressure buildup and possible injury. Store them with Sip & Seal Lids instead.

Autumn Latte Lifter

Servings:3-4
Cooking Time:x

Ingredients:

- 2 tablespoons espresso powder,
- 1/4 cup pumpkin puree,
- 3 tablespoons maple syrup,
- 1/8 teaspoon ground cloves,
- 1 cup low-fat milk,
- 2 cups vanilla nonfat frozen yogurt,
- 1 1/2 cups ice cubes

Directions:

1. Place the Top Blades in the Pitcher and add all of the ingredients in the order listed.*
2. Select Speed 1 and flip the switch to START. Slowly increase to Speed 6 and blend until smooth.

Fresh Tomato Bloody Mary

Servings:x
Cooking Time:x

Ingredients:

- 3 ripe tomatoes, quartered
- 4 ounces vodka
- 2 teaspoons lemon juice
- 1 teaspoon horseradish
- 1 teaspoon Worcestershire sauce
- 1/2 teaspoon celery seed
- 1/2 teaspoon freshly ground black pepper
- 1/2 teaspoon salt
- Ice
- Extra-large green olives on wooden skewers, for garnish
- Fresh ribs celery with leaves, for garnish

Directions:

1. Using the Bottom Blades in the Pitcher, add tomatoes. PULSE 5 times.
2. Pour juice through a fine mesh strainer. Return to Pitcher and add all of the remaining ingredients in the order listed, except ice and garnishes.
3. Select Speed 3 and flip the switch to START. Slowly increase to Speed 8 and blend until smooth.
4. Divide between ice-filled glasses and garnish each with olives and celery.

Gremolata

Servings:x
Cooking Time:x

Ingredients:

- 3 tablespoons olive oil
- 1 1/2 cups flat-leaf parsley leaves, minced
- 1 tablespoon lemon juice
- 1 1/2 teaspoons lemon zest
- Salt and pepper to taste

Directions:

1. Mince parsley in Nutri Ninja
2. cup by pulsing until desired consistency. Remove the blades from the cup after blending. Combine parsley with olive oil, lemon juice and lemon zest. Add salt and pepper to taste.
3. Go ahead, embrace your inner meal prepper. We hear you, blending the night before is a huge time saver. But, heads up, never store your creation with the blade assembly attached—active ingredients in some foods may lead to pressure buildup and possible injury. Store them with Sip & Seal Lids instead.
4. Use as a garnish in our recipe for
5. Asparagus and Watercress Soup with White Beans

Tranquil Peach Cream

Servings:1
Cooking Time:x

Ingredients:

- 1 peach, pitted (peeled if desired),
- 1 tangerine, peeled,
- 1 banana, peeled, cut in half,
- 2 tablespoons hemp seeds,
- 3/4 cup vanilla almond milk,
- 3 to 4 ice cubes

Directions:

1. Place all of the ingredients into the Nutri Ninja cup in the order listed. PULSE until smooth. Remove the blades from the cup after blending.
2. Go ahead, embrace your inner meal prepper. We hear you, making smoothies the night before is a huge time saver. But, heads up, never store your smoothies with the blade assembly attached—active ingredients in some foods may lead to pressure buildup and possible injury. Store them with Sip & Seal Lids instead.

Chillout Chai Smoothie

Servings:2-4
Cooking Time:x

Ingredients:

- 2 ripe bananas,
- 2 cups chai tea,
- 1/2 cup soy milk,
- 3 cups ice cubes

Directions:

1. Place the Top Blades in the Pitcher and add all of the ingredients in the order listed.
2. PULSE 3 times. Select Speed 10 and flip the switch to START. Blend for 45 seconds.

Tomato Basil Soup

Servings:4 (8-ounce)
Cooking Time:15–20 Minutes

Ingredients:

- 1 clove garlic
- 1 can (28 ounces) crushed tomatoes
- 1/2 cup fresh basil
- 1 cup low-sodium vegetable broth
- 2 tablespoons tomato paste
- 1/4 teaspoon salt
- 1/4 teaspoon ground black pepper

Directions:

1. Place all ingredients into the 72-ounce Pitcher in the order listed.
2. Select HIGH and blend until smooth, about 1 minute.
3. Pour soup into a medium saucepan and simmer 15 to 20 minutes.
4. Go ahead, embrace your inner meal prepper. We hear you, making smoothies the night before is a huge time saver. But, heads up, never store your smoothies with the blade assembly attached—active ingredients in some foods may lead to pressure buildup and possible injury. Store them with Sip & Seal Lids instead.

Cantaloupe Pepper Freeze

Servings:4-6
Cooking Time:x

Ingredients:

- 1/2 cantaloupe, chunked and frozen, (about 2 cups),
- 1/2 teaspoon freshly ground black pepper,
- 3/4 to 1 1/2 cups water, divided,
- 1 cup ice cubes

Directions:

1. Place the Top Blades in the Pitcher and add ice, cantaloupe, pepper and 3/4 cup water. PULSE 3 times. Add additional water if needed.
2. Select Speed 3 and flip the switch to START. Slowly increase to Speed 8 and process until smooth.
3. Serve immediately or transfer to a shallow glass baking dish and freeze to desired consistency.

Best Blender Salsa

Servings:makes About 4 Cups.

Cooking Time:x

Ingredients:

- 2 10-ounce cans tomatoes (see tip below),
- 1 white onion, peeled and quartered,
- 1 jalapeño pepper, seeded,
- 1 canned chipotle chile pepper, with 2 tablespoons adobo sauce,
- 1 bunch cilantro, stems trimmed,
- 1 lime, peeled and quartered,
- salt and pepper to taste

Directions:

1. Place the Top Blades in the Pitcher and add all of the ingredients in the order listed.
2. PULSE until chunky consistency is achieved.
3. Cover and refrigerate for at least 1 hour before serving.
4. Go ahead, embrace your inner meal prepper. We hear you, making smoothies the night before is a huge time saver. But, heads up, never store your smoothies with the blade assembly attached—active ingredients in some foods may lead to pressure buildup and possible injury. Store them with Sip & Seal Lids instead.

Vegan Butternut Squash Soup

Servings:3-4
Cooking Time:30-35 Minutes

Ingredients:

- 3 tablespoons olive oil,
- 1 large yellow onion, chopped,
- 1 cup raw cashews,
- 2 pounds butternut squash, cubed,
- 1 large apple, peeled, cored and chopped (honey crisp or braeburn),
- 1 cup carrot, chopped,
- 1 teaspoon fresh thyme leaves,
- 1 bay leaf,
- 4 cups vegetable stock, plus more to thin if desired,
- 1/2 teaspoon Kosher salt, plus more to taste,
- Black pepper, to taste

Directions:

1. Set Ninja Cooking System to STOVETOP HIGH or use a large skillet pan. Add oil and heat until it shimmers. Add the onions and cook, stirring, until they begin to soften, about 5 minutes.
2. Add the cashews and cook, stirring, until the onions are translucent and the cashews have slightly browned, about 3 minutes.
3. Add the squash, apple, carrot, thyme, and bay leaf and sauté for 5 minutes. Add the stock and stir to combine. Season to taste with salt and pepper and bring the soup to a simmer. Reduce the heat to MED, cover the pot and cook the soup until the squash is easily pierced with a knife, 20 to 25 minutes.
4. Remove and discard bay leaf. Let soup cool to room temperature.
5. Place the Top Blades in the Ninja Ultima Pitcher and select Speed 1. Working in batches, pour cooled soup into Pitcher. Flip the switch to START and slowly increase to Speed 7 and blend for 30 seconds or until the soup reaches a creamy, silky texture. Repeat with remaining soup.*
6. Add all blended soup to the Ninja Cooking System or large stock pot and reheat on STOVETOP MED. Season to taste with salt and pepper before serving.

World's Best Cheeseburgers

Servings:4
Cooking Time:15 Minutes

Ingredients:

- 3/4 pound beef chuck, trimmed, cut into large chunks and well-chilled,
- 1/4 pound beef sirloin, cut into large chunks and well-chilled,
- 1 1/2 teaspoons salt,
- 1/2 teaspoon black pepper,
- 4 slices cheddar cheese,
- 4 whole wheat hamburger buns, warmed,
- 4 tablespoons mayonnaise (use regular or low-fat),
- 4 slices ripe tomato,
- 4 to 8 romaine lettuce leaves,
- 4 slices sweet white onion

Directions:

1. Place the Top Blades in the Pitcher and add the beef, salt and pepper. PULSE to a fine chop. Do not overprocess.
2. Remove beef from Pitcher and lightly form into 4 patties. Do not handle the meat more than necessary.
3. Cook patties on a hot grill to your preference, about 4 to 5 minutes per side for rare, 5 to 6 minutes per side for medium and 6 to 7 minutes per side for well-done.
4. Turn the patties once while grilling, topping each with a slice of cheese after turning.
5. Place the patties on warmed buns. Garnish each cheeseburger with mayonnaise, tomatoes, lettuce and onions.

Collard Green Pesto Sauce

Servings:makes 16 Ounces
Cooking Time:2 Minutes

Ingredients:

- 1 bunch collard greens, with ribs removed
- 8 large pitted green olives
- 1/2 cup olive oil
- 1/4 cup walnuts
- 2 tablespoons cider vinegar
- 1/2 teaspoon honey
- 1/4 teaspoon red pepper
- Kosher salt and pepper

Directions:

1. Set up a large bowl with ice water. Blanch collard greens by immersing in salted boiling water for 2 minutes. Remove greens and place in ice water to stop cooking and cool. Drain greens and squeeze out water.
2. Add greens to the Ninja food processor fitted with the steel quad blade. Add olives, oil, walnuts, cider vinegar, honey and red pepper flakes. Process until desired consistency. Taste, season with salt and pepper and adjust flavors as desired.
3. Go ahead, embrace your inner meal prepper. We hear you, making smoothies the night before is a huge time saver. But, heads up, never store your smoothies with the blade assembly attached—active ingredients in some foods may lead to pressure buildup and possible injury. Store them with Sip & Seal Lids instead.

Eyeball Smoothie

Servings:4
Cooking Time:x

Ingredients:

- 2 kiwis, peeled and thinly sliced (1/8") across center in disks, measuring 1" in diameter
- 1-.67 ounce tube of black cake decorating gel writer
- 1-.67 ounce tube of red cake decorating gel writer
- 1/4 cup coconut milk
- 1 cup plain low-fat yogurt
- 2 cups frozen pineapple
- 1 cup almond milk
- 1 1/2 cups ice

Directions:

1. Prepare 8 eyeballs, 2 for each serving, by squeezing a small circle of black gel onto center of kiwi to form iris. Drizzle red gel around iris to form the blood shot in eyes; set aside.
2. Place the Top Blades in the Ninja Ultima Pitcher. Add coconut milk, yogurt, pineapple, almond milk and ice to the Pitcher.
3. PULSE 3 times. Select Speed 8 and flip the switch to START. Blend for 45 seconds or until smooth.*
4. Pour smoothie into 4 individual wide mouth glasses. With a flat spatula or wide knife, place 2 eyeballs in each glass. Serve immediately.

Pineapple Cilantro Dipping Sauce

Servings:x
Cooking Time:x

Ingredients:

- 1 cup pineapple
- 1/2 small serrano chile, seeded
- 1/2 sweet white onion, peeled, cut in half
- 2 tablespoons cilantro leaves
- 2 tablespoons lime juice
- 1 tablespoon coconut oil or other oil
- salt and pepper to taste

Directions:

1. Place all of the ingredients into the Nutri Ninja Cup in the order listed. PULSE until smooth. Remove the blades from the cup after blending. Season with salt and pepper and serve or refrigerate covered for up to 2 days.
2. Go ahead, embrace your inner meal prepper. We hear you, making smoothies the night before is a huge time saver. But, heads up, never store your smoothies with the blade assembly attached—active ingredients in some foods may lead to pressure buildup and possible injury. Store them with Sip Seal Lids instead.

Lean Green Ninja

Servings:2-4
Cooking Time:x

Ingredients:

- 1 cup pineapple, 1-inch chunks,
- 1 cup mango, 1-inch chunks,
- 1 small banana,
- 1/2 cup packed spinach,
- 1/2 cup packed kale,
- 1/2 cup water,
- 1 cup ice

Directions:

1. Place the Top Blades in the Pitcher and add all of the ingredients in the order listed.*
2. PULSE 3 times. Select Speed 10 and flip the switch to START. Blend for 45 seconds.
3. Go ahead, embrace your inner meal prepper. We hear you, making smoothies the night before is a huge time saver. But, heads up, never store your smoothies with the blade assembly attached—active ingredients in some foods may lead to pressure buildup and possible injury. Store them with Sip & Seal Lids instead.

Cranberry Orange Cake

Servings:x
Cooking Time:x

Ingredients:

- 2 1/2 cups all-purpose white flour
- 2 teaspoons baking powder
- 1/2 teaspoon baking soda
- 1/2 teaspoon salt
- 1 cup brown sugar
- 1/4 cup granulated sugar
- 1/2 cup butter, melted and cooled to room temperature
- 1/2 cup low-fat sour cream
- 1/4 cup orange juice
- 3 eggs
- 1 teaspoon vanilla extract
- 1 cup dried cranberries, chopped and soaked in 1/2 cup orange liqueur
- 1/2 cup pecans, toasted
- cooking spray

Directions:

1. In a large bowl, combine flour, baking powder, baking soda and salt and set aside.
2. Using the Bottom Blades in the Pitcher, add the remaining ingredients, except the cranberries and pecans. Select Speed 1 and flip the switch to START. Slowly increase to Speed 5 and blend until well-combined.
3. Pour the sour cream/egg mixture into the flour mixture in the bowl, stirring well to incorporate. Drain cranberries and add into the batter. Add the toasted pecans and stir.
4. Lightly coat a 9 x 5-inch loaf pan with cooking spray. Pour batter into pan and bake at 350°F for 50 to 60 minutes until a knife inserted into center comes out clean.

Emerald Isle Chicken

Servings:6
Cooking Time:1 Hour

Ingredients:
- 1 small bunch parsley
- 2 garlic cloves
- 1 large shallot
- 1 tablespoon herbes de Provence spice blend
- 1 sprig fresh rosemary, stemmed
- 1 1/2 tablespoons Dijon-style mustard
- 1 teaspoon Kosher salt
- 1 teaspoon black pepper
- 1/4 cup plus 1 tablespoon olive oil
- Grated zest of 1 lemon
- 3 pounds bone-in chicken thighs (skin removed if desired) or boneless, skinless chicken breast

Directions:
1. Place parsley, garlic, shallot, herbes de Provence, rosemary, mustard, salt, pepper and olive oil into the Single Serve. Blend for 45 seconds or until smooth. Remove the blades from the cup after blending. Stir in lemon zest. Slather green paste all over chicken.
2. Set the Cooking System to OVEN 375*F for 1 hour. Place chicken into pot. Pour sauce from Single Serve over chicken. Cover and cook for 1 hour or until chicken is cooked through (165*F).

Powerhouse Green Smoothie

Servings:1 12-ounce
Cooking Time:x

Ingredients:

- 1/2 cup green cabbage, coarsely chopped
- 1/2 cup kale
- 1/2 small green apple, quartered
- 6 green grapes
- 1/2 cup almond milk
- 1 tablespoon lemon juice
- 10 mint leaves
- 4 ice cubes

Directions:

1. Add all ingredients in order listed into the Single Serve and process until smooth. Remove the blades from the cup after blending.
2. Go ahead, embrace your inner meal prepper. We hear you, making smoothies the night before is a huge time saver. But, heads up, never store your smoothies with the blade assembly attached—active ingredients in some foods may lead to pressure buildup and possible injury. Store them with Sip Seal Lids instead.

Chocolate Pecan Pie Smoothie

Servings:4 8-ounce
Cooking Time:x

Ingredients:

- 1 cup pecans,
- 2 tablespoons unsweetened cocoa powder,
- 3 tablespoons Golden Syrup or agave,
- 1/2 teaspoon salt,
- 1 1/2 cups almond milk,
- 2 teaspoons vanilla,
- 1/4 teaspoon cinnamon,
- 1 1/2 cups ice

Directions:

1. Using the Bottom Blades in the Ninja Ultima Pitcher, add the pecans and PULSE to finely chop.
2. Add cocoa powder, golden syrup, and salt and PULSE 5 times. Select Speed 3 and flip the switch to START. Slowly increase to Speed 8 and blend until smooth, scraping down the sides as necessary.
3. Add almond milk, vanilla, cinnamon and ice to Pitcher. Select Speed 3 and flip the switch to START. Slowly increase to Speed 8.

Turkey Meatballs

Servings:makes About 30 Mini Meatballs.
Cooking Time:20 Minutes

Ingredients:

- 1 pound dark turkey meat, cut into 1-inch cubes and well-chilled,
- 1/2 onion, peeled and chopped,
- 3 cloves garlic, peeled and minced,
- 1/4 cup Italian parsley leaves, chopped, plus more for garnish,
- 1/2 cup Parmesan cheese, grated,
- 1/4 cup bread crumbs,
- 2 tablespoons tomato paste,
- 1 egg, beaten,
- salt and pepper to taste,
- cooking spray,
- 4 cups jarred marinara sauce

Directions:

1. Place Top Blades in the Pitcher and add turkey. PULSE to a fine chop. Do not overprocess.
2. Transfer to bowl and add onion, garlic, parsley, cheese, bread crumbs, tomato paste, egg, salt and pepper, mixing to combine. Form mixture into mini meatballs.
3. Lightly coat a large skillet with cooking spray. Over medium-high heat, sauté meatballs until browned on all sides, about 5 minutes. Add marinara sauce and simmer until sauce is thickened and meatballs are cooked through completely, about 15 to 20 minutes.
4. Serve over cooked pasta or as an appetizer garnished with chopped parsley.
5. Go ahead, embrace your inner meal prepper. We hear you, making smoothies the night before is a huge time saver. But, heads up, never store your smoothies with the blade assembly attached—active ingredients in some foods may lead to pressure buildup and possible injury. Store them with Sip & Seal Lids instead.

Citrus Ginger Super Juice

Servings:1-2
Cooking Time:x

Ingredients:

- 1 cup frozen mango chunks,
- 1 pink grapefruit, peeled and quartered,
- 1 orange, peeled and quartered,
- 1 lime, juiced,
- 1/2-inch piece of ginger, peeled,
- 1/2 cup ice cubes

Directions:

1. Place the Top Blades in the Pitcher and add all of the ingredients in the order listed.*
2. Select Speed 1 and flip the switch to START. Slowly increase to Speed 8 and blend until smooth.
3. Go ahead, embrace your inner meal prepper. We hear you, making smoothies the night before is a huge time saver. But, heads up, never store your smoothies with the blade assembly attached—active ingredients in some foods may lead to pressure buildup and possible injury. Store them with Sip & Seal Lids instead.

Kale And Cabbage Slaw

Servings:4
Cooking Time:x

Ingredients:

- 1/2 head red cabbage, trimmed, cut into pieces,
- 1 bunch kale, thick stems removed, quartered,
- 1 stalk broccoli, trimmed, cut into pieces,
- 1/2 cup golden raisins,
- 1/2 cup almonds, toasted and chopped.
- Dressing:
- 1/4 cup low-fat sour cream,
- 1/4 cup low-fat mayonnaise,
- 1 tablespoon apple cider vinegar,
- 1 tablespoon honey,
- 2 teaspoons poppy seeds,
- salt and pepper to taste

Directions:

1. Place the Top Blades in the Pitcher and add cabbage, kale and broccoli. If needed, work in batches. PULSE to roughly chop.
2. Transfer to a large bowl, add raisins and almonds and set aside.
3. Place remaining ingredients into the Single Serve Cup and PULSE until smooth.
4. Remove the blades from the cup after blending.
5. Pour dressing over vegetable mixture and toss to coat. Serve or refrigerate until ready to serve.

Seeded Snack Bars

Servings:16
Cooking Time:x

Ingredients:

- 3/4 cup toasted rolled oats
- 9 dates
- 1/2 cup pumpkin seeds
- 1/2 cup sunflower seeds
- 1/4 cup dried cherries
- 2 tablespoons hemp seeds
- 1 tablespoon sesame seeds
- 1 tablespoon flax seeds
- 3 tablespoons coconut flakes
- 1/4 cup semisweet chocolate chips
- 3 tablespoons sunflower butter
- 1 tablespoon maple syrup
- 2 tablespoons water
- 1/2 teaspoon sea salt

Directions:

1. Combine all ingredients into the Ninja Ultima Pitcher.
2. Pulse until well combined, scraping down Pitcher as necessary.
3. Line an 8x8-inch pan with plastic wrap and spread the mixture evenly, pressing down.
4. Chill for at least one hour, remove from pan and cut into 16 portions.

Superfood Snack Bars

Servings:12
Cooking Time:x

Ingredients:

- 1 cup raw almonds,
- 8 pitted dates,
- 1/4 cup dried cherries,
- 2 tablespoons unsweetened coconut flakes,
- 1 tablespoon hemp seeds,
- 2 teaspoons maple syrup,
- 2 tablespoons toasted pumpkin seeds,
- 1 tablespoon water

Directions:

1. Using the Bottom Blade in the pitcher, add all ingredients except pumpkin seeds and water.
2. PULSE 8-10 times, until the dates have been broken down and the mixture is coarsely chopped.
3. Remove lid and carefully scrape down sides. Add pumpkin seeds and water. PULSE 3 more times until mixture is uniform.
4. Spray a small baking dish with non-stick spray, and spoon the mixture into the pan, pressing it down.
5. Refrigerate for at least an hour before cutting into bars and serving.
6. Go ahead, embrace your inner meal prepper. We hear you, making smoothies the night before is a huge time saver. But, heads up, never store your smoothies with the blade assembly attached—active ingredients in some foods may lead to pressure buildup and possible injury. Store them with Sip & Seal Lids instead.

Heart-y Roasted Red Pepper Dip

Servings:about 4 Cups.

Cooking Time:x

Ingredients:

- 2 12-ounce jars roasted red pepper, drained
- 4 canned chipotle peppers with 2 tablespoons adobo sauce, or more to taste
- 2 cups almonds, blanched
- 2 cloves garlic, peeled
- Salt and pepper to taste

Directions:

1. Place all the ingredients in the order listed into a Ninja 72-ounce Pitcher and blend on Medium Speed for 45 seconds or until smooth.
2. Refrigerate for at least 1 hour before servings.

Roasted Cauliflower Fettuccine Alfredo

Servings:x
Cooking Time:x

Ingredients:

- 1 cauliflower head, cut into 2-inch florets
- 1/2 onion, peeled, cut in half
- 2 tablespoons olive oil
- Salt and pepper to taste
- 1 1/2 cups low-fat milk
- 2 cups Parmesan cheese, grated
- 1/8 teaspoon ground nutmeg
- 1 pound fettuccine noodles, cooked, kept warm
- 2 tablespoons fresh parsley, chopped

Directions:

1. Toss cauliflower and onion with oil, salt and pepper and roast in a shallow baking pan at 375°F for 25 minutes, until tender and lightly browned. Cool to room temperature.
2. Using the Bottom Blades in the Pitcher, add the cooled vegetables and milk. PULSE 3 times. Add the cheese, select Speed 1 and flip the switch to START. Slowly increase to Speed 6 and blend until smooth.
3. Pour sauce into saucepan, add nutmeg and simmer until heated through, about 10 minutes.
4. Toss with fettuccine and serve hot, garnished with parsley.

Sweet Beet Clarifier

Servings:1-2
Cooking Time:x

Ingredients:

- 1 beet, raw, peeled, chunked,
- 2 carrots, scrubbed, cut in half,
- 1 apple, cored, cut in half,
- 3/4 cup water,
- 5 to 6 ice cubes

Directions:

1. Place the Top Blades in the Pitcher and add all of the ingredients in the order listed.*
2. Select Speed 1 and flip the switch to START. Slowly increase to Speed 8 and blend until smooth.

Walnut Red Pepper Dip

Servings:2 Cups
Cooking Time:x

Ingredients:

- 1 jar (7 ounces) roasted red peppers
- 1/4 (6-inch) round pita bread
- 1 cup toasted walnuts
- 2 tablespoons fresh lemon juice
- 2 tablespoons tomato paste
- 1/4 teaspoon red pepper flakes
- 1 teaspoon ground cumin
- 1/4 cup olive oil
- 1/8 teaspoon salt
- Pinch ground black pepper
- Cut vegetables and pita chips, for dipping

Directions:

1. Drain peppers and reserve liquid in a small bowl. Tear pita bread in 1-inch pieces and place in bowl of liquid to soften, about 3 minutes.
2. Place softened pita bread and remaining ingredients, except cut vegetables and pita chips, into the 24-ounce Tritan Nutri Ninja.
3. PULSE 3 times, then select START/STOP and blend until smooth. Remove the blades from the cup after blending. Transfer dip to a serving bowl. Serve with cut vegetables and pita chips.
4. Go ahead, embrace your inner meal prepper. We hear you, making smoothies the night before is a huge time saver. But, heads up, never store your smoothies with the blade assembly attached—active ingredients in some foods may lead to pressure buildup and possible injury. Store them with Sip & Seal Lids instead.

Watermelon Raspberry Cleanser

Servings:1-2
Cooking Time:x

Ingredients:

- 3 cups watermelon, cut in chunks,
- 1 cup raspberries,
- 1/2 cup water,
- 1 cup ice cubes

Directions:

1. Place the Top Blades in the Pitcher and add all of the ingredients in the order listed.*
2. Select Speed 1 and flip the switch to START. Slowly increase to Speed 8 and blend until smooth.
3. Go ahead, embrace your inner meal prepper. We hear you, making smoothies the night before is a huge time saver. But, heads up, never store your smoothies with the blade assembly attached—active ingredients in some foods may lead to pressure buildup and possible injury. Store them with Sip & Seal Lids instead.

Pumpkin Pie Smoothie

Servings:4 8-ounce
Cooking Time:x

Ingredients:

- 16 ounces lite silken tofu,
- 3 tablespoons Golden Syrup or brown sugar,
- 1 cup pumpkin pie mix,
- 1/2 teaspoon pumpkin pie spice,
- Pinch nutmeg,
- 1/4 teaspoon salt,
- 2 cups ice

Directions:

1. Place the Top Blades in the Ninja Ultima Pitcher and add all of the ingredients in the order listed.
2. PULSE 3 times. Select Speed 10 and flip the switch to START. Blend for 45 seconds or until smooth. Taste and adjust spices as desired.

Cucumber Citrus Margarita

Servings:4 (8-ounce)
Cooking Time:x

Ingredients:

- 1/4 cucumber, peeled
- 1/2 orange, peeled
- 1 lime, peeled, cut in half
- 1 lemon, peeled, cut in quarters
- 1/4 cup triple sec
- 2/3 cup tequila
- 1 tablespoon honey
- 4 cups ice, divided

Directions:

1. Place all ingredients into the 72-ounce Pitcher in the order listed.
2. Press Auto-iQ BLEND.
3. Go ahead, embrace your inner meal prepper. We hear you, making smoothies the night before is a huge time saver. But, heads up, never store your smoothies with the blade assembly attached—active ingredients in some foods may lead to pressure buildup and possible injury. Store them with Sip & Seal Lids instead.

Guacamole Graveyard

Servings:6
Cooking Time:x

Ingredients:
- 1/2 small red onion
- 4 ripe avocados
- Juice of 2 limes
- 1/2 teaspoon cumin
- 1/4 teaspoon cayenne
- 1/4 cup chopped cilantro
- Kosher salt and pepper to taste
- 7-Grain Sea Salt crackers, or any other rectangle crackers as desired
- Black cake decorating gel writer

Directions:
1. Cut avocados in half by inserting a knife down the center until it touches the pit, then carefully rotate the avocado until it is sliced through on all sides. Separate the two halves, remove the pit and discard. Use a spoon to scoop the pulp out, tracing along the inner skin of the avocado.
2. Place the Top Blades in the Ninja Ultima Pitcher and add all of the ingredients in the order listed.
3. PULSE 12-14 times, scraping down bowl if necessary.
4. Place guacamole in a medium sized serving dish. Write "R.I.P.", "BOO" or your favorite Halloween saying with black gel writer on a few crackers and place in dip like tombstones. Serve with additional crackers.

Apricot-mustard Dressing

Servings:1 3/4 Cups
Cooking Time:x

Ingredients:

- 2 tablespoons fresh thyme leaves
- 2 tablespoons Dijon mustard
- 1/4 cup rice wine vinegar
- 3/4 cup nonfat sour cream
- 3 tablespoons olive oil
- 3 tablespoons honey
- 1/2 cup apricot jam
- 1/2 teaspoon salt

Directions:

1. Place all ingredients into the 24-ounce Nutri Ninja in the order listed.
2. Select HIGH and blend for 30 seconds.
3. Remove the blades from the cup after blending.
4. Go ahead, embrace your inner meal prepper. We hear you, making smoothies the night before is a huge time saver. But, heads up, never store your smoothies with the blade assembly attached—active ingredients in some foods may lead to pressure buildup and possible injury. Store them with Sip & Seal Lids instead.

Whole Lemon Tart With Pistachio Crust

Servings:6-8
Cooking Time:35 Minutes

Ingredients:

- 1 cup pistachios,
- 1/2 cup all-purpose flour,
- 1/4 cup sugar,
- 1/4 teaspoon salt,
- 1/2 stick butter, melted,
- 1/2 teaspoon vanilla,
- Non-stick cooking spray,
- 1 lemon, organic or washed, coarsely chopped and seeds removed,
- 1 cup sugar,
- 3 tablespoons lemon juice,
- 3 large eggs,
- 4 tablespoons butter, melted,
- Powdered sugar

Directions:

1. Preheat to 350°F. Place the Top Blades in the Ninja Ultima Pitcher and add pistachios. PULSE until finely ground. Pour pistachio flour and all-purpose flour into a medium bowl and add sugar, salt, butter and vanilla. Stir with a fork until fully incorporated. Lightly coat and 8" tart pan with non-stick cooking spray and press crust mixture into pan. Bake for 13-15 minutes, or until lightly golden brown.
2. Reduce heat to 300°F. Place lemon, sugar, lemon juice, eggs and melted butter into the Pitcher.
3. Select Speed 1. Flip the switch to START and slowly increase to Speed 9. Blend for 45 seconds or until smooth.*
4. Pour lemon mixture oven into crust and bake for 20 minutes or until just set in center. Let cool. Place powdered sugar in a fine sieve and dust top. Store in refrigerator.

Crushed Peppermint Frozen Frappe

Servings:4
Cooking Time:x

Ingredients:

- 4 cups vanilla low-fat vanilla frozen yogurt,
- 1 cup almond milk,
- 1/2 cup peppermint candies (about 25),
- Peppermint sticks for garnish

Directions:

1. Place the Top Blades in the Ninja Ultima Pitcher. Add frozen yogurt, almond milk and peppermint candies to the Pitcher.
2. PULSE 3 times. Select Speed 8 and flip the switch to START. Blend for 45 seconds or until smooth.*
3. Serve in small glasses topped with a peppermint stick.
4. Go ahead, embrace your inner meal prepper. We hear you, making smoothies the night before is a huge time saver. But, heads up, never store your smoothies with the blade assembly attached—active ingredients in some foods may lead to pressure buildup and possible injury. Store them with Sip & Seal Lids instead.

Spicy Pineapple Recharge

Servings:4-5
Cooking Time:x

Ingredients:
- 1 small pineapple, peeled and chunked,
- 2 tablespoons fresh ginger, peeled,
- 2 limes, peeled and quartered,
- 1 small jalapeño pepper, seeded,
- 1 1/2 cups orange juice,
- 1 cup ice cubes

Directions:
1. Place the Top Blades in the Pitcher and add all of the ingredients in the order listed.*
2. PULSE 3 times. Select Speed 10 and flip the switch to START. Blend for 45 seconds.
3. Go ahead, embrace your inner meal prepper. We hear you, making smoothies the night before is a huge time saver. But, heads up, never store your smoothies with the blade assembly attached—active ingredients in some foods may lead to pressure buildup and possible injury. Store them with Sip & Seal Lids instead.

Butternut Squash Mac And Cheese

Servings:4-6
Cooking Time:45 Minutes

Ingredients:

- 1 pound butternut squash, peeled and cut into large pieces,
- 1 cup water,
- 1 cup low-fat milk,
- salt and pepper to taste,
- 1 teaspoon dry mustard powder,
- 3 cups cheddar cheese, shredded, divided,
- 8 ounces elbow macaroni, cooked,
- 1/4 cup bread crumbs,
- 1/4 cup Parmesan cheese, grated,
- 2 teaspoons olive oil

Directions:

1. Place the Top Blades in the Pitcher and add the squash and water. PULSE to chop.
2. In a saucepan, place the squash, water, milk, salt, pepper and mustard. Simmer for 20 minutes. Add 2 1/2 cups cheese and stir until melted. Cool until just warm.
3. Using the Bottom Blades in the Pitcher, add the cooled mixture. Select Speed 1 and flip the switch to START. Slowly increase to Speed 5 and process until smooth.
4. Place cooked macaroni in a lightly buttered 2 1/2-quart baking dish. Pour squash mixture over macaroni. Toss bread crumbs, remaining cheddar cheese, Parmesan cheese and oil and scatter over top.
5. Bake at 375°F for 20 to 25 minutes, until bubbly.

Pot O' Gold Cauliflower Soup

Servings:4-6
Cooking Time:35 Minutes

Ingredients:

- 1 tablespoon coconut oil
- 1 yellow onion, peeled and chopped coarsely
- 1 head cauliflower, chopped
- 5 cups vegetable stock
- 1 teaspoon turmeric
- 1/2 teaspoon ground mustard
- 1 teaspoon cumin
- 1/2 teaspoon cayenne
- Kosher salt and pepper to taste
- For garnish, 1 large lime and 1/4 cup cilantro, chopped

Directions:

1. Set the Cooking System to STOVETOP MEDIUM. Heat coconut oil and add onions and cook for 3-5 minutes or until softened. Add cauliflower to pot and cook for 5 minutes.
2. Add vegetable stock, turmeric, ground mustard, cumin and cayenne. Set to STOVETOP HIGH and bring to a boil. Turn down to STOVETOP LOW and simmer for 20-25 minutes or until cauliflower is softened. Let cool completely.
3. Add half of soup into Blender pitcher. Blend on High for 45 seconds or until smooth. Season with salt and pepper to taste.
4. To garnish, squeeze lime juice on top of soup in individual bowls and sprinkle with cilantro.

Skinny Belly Busting Breakfast Replacement Smoothie

Servings:4 14-ounce
Cooking Time:x

Ingredients:

- 4 bananas
- 2 cups low-fat plain Greek Yogurt
- 4 tablespoons flax seed
- 3 cups green tea
- 2 cups frozen strawberries
- 4 teaspoons agave

Directions:

1. Place TOP BLADES in the Ninja Ultima Pitcher and add all ingredients in order listed. PULSE 3 times and flip the switch to START. Set to Speed 1 and slowly increase to Speed 8. Blend for 45 seconds or until smooth.

Cream Of Broccoli Soup

Servings:x
Cooking Time:x

Ingredients:

- 1 cup raw cashews, soaked in water for 2 hours, drained
- 4 cups vegetable broth, divided
- 6 cups broccoli, steamed
- 1 teaspoon garlic powder
- salt and pepper to taste

Directions:

1. Place the Top Blades in the Pitcher and add the cashews and 1/2 cup broth. PULSE 5 times.
2. Add remaining ingredients and Select Speed 3 and flip the switch to START. Slowly increase to Speed 10 and blend until smooth, about 30 seconds.
3. Transfer soup to a stockpot, adjust seasonings and simmer until heated through.

Irish Toddy Slush

Servings:x
Cooking Time:x

Ingredients:

- 1/2 cup prepared black tea, chilled
- 1/4 cup low-fat milk
- 2 tablespoons agave or honey
- 2 tablespoons lemon juice
- 1/4 teaspoon ground cardamom
- 2 ounces Irish whiskey
- 1 cup ice
- Walnuts or chocolate for garnish if desired

Directions:

1. Place all of the ingredients in the Nutri Ninja
2. Cup in the order listed. PULSE until smooth. Remove the blades from the cup after blending.
3. Go ahead, embrace your inner meal prepper. We hear you, making smoothies the night before is a huge time saver. But, heads up, never store your smoothies with the blade assembly attached—active ingredients in some foods may lead to pressure buildup and possible injury. Store them with Sip & Seal Lids instead.

Heart Healthy Green Smoothie

Servings:4
Cooking Time:x

Ingredients:

- 4 dates, pitted
- 2 stalks celery, cut into quarters
- 2 ripe kiwis, peeled, cut in half
- 2 cups cabbage, chopped
- 2 cups kale
- 2 2/3 cups almond milk
- 2 cups ice

Directions:

1. Soak the dates in 2 cups warm water for 30 minutes. Drain. Set aside.
2. Place all the ingredients in the order listed into a Ninja 72-ounce Pitcher and blend on High Speed for 45 seconds or until fully blended.

Antioxidant Refresher

Servings:2
Cooking Time:x

Ingredients:

- 1/4 cup red cabbage,
- 1 stalk celery, halved,
- 1 apple, halved,
- 3/4 cup blueberries,
- 1/2 cup watermelon,
- 2 cups ice

Directions:

1. Place the Top Blades in the Pitcher and add all of the ingredients in the order listed.*
2. PULSE 3 times. Select Speed 10 and flip the switch to START. Blend for 45 seconds.
3. Go ahead, embrace your inner meal prepper. We hear you, making smoothies the night before is a huge time saver. But, heads up, never store your smoothies with the blade assembly attached—active ingredients in some foods may lead to pressure buildup and possible injury. Store them with Sip & Seal Lids instead.

Chilled Apple Pear Sauce

Servings:4-6
Cooking Time:20 Minutes

Ingredients:
- 4 apples, peeled, cored and cut in quarters,
- 2 pears, peeled, cored and cut in quarters,
- 1/4 cup sugar,
- 1/2 cup water

Directions:
1. Place the Top Blades in the Ninja Ultima Pitcher and add the apples and pears.
2. PULSE 3 times. Scrape down sides if necessary.
3. Select Speed 3 and flip switch to START. Blend for 10 seconds or until smooth.*
4. Place pureed fruit into the Ninja Cooking System pot. Add water and sugar and set to STOVETOP MEDIUM. Bring to a simmer for 15 minutes, stirring to prevent sticking. Allow to cool and place in the refrigerator. Serve chilled.

Valentine's Day Cherry Cordial Smoothie

Servings:4
Cooking Time:x

Ingredients:

- 1 ripe avocado, pitted
- 3 cups unsweetened almond milk
- 1 1/2 cups frozen cherries
- 4 tablespoons unsweetened cocoa powder
- 1 1/4 cups tart cherry juice
- 2 1/2 tablespoons agave

Directions:

1. Place all the ingredients in the order listed into a Ninja 72-ounce Pitcher and blend on High Speed for 45 seconds or until smooth.

Greek Olivada

Servings:6-8
Cooking Time:x

Ingredients:

- 2 cups kalamata olives, pitted,
- 1 clove garlic, peeled, chopped,
- 2 tablespoons extra-virgin olive oil,
- 1 teaspoon lemon zest,
- 2 tablespoons lemon juice,
- 1/4 teaspoon fennel seeds,
- Salt and pepper to taste

Directions:

1. Place the Top Blades in the Ninja Ultima Pitcher and add all of the ingredients in the order listed.
2. PULSE to a rough chop, scraping down the sides as necessary.
3. Transfer to a serving bowl and serve at room temperature.

Sunflower Seed Butter

Servings:x

Cooking Time:x

Ingredients:

- 8 ounces roasted, unsalted sunflower seeds
- 1 tablespoon sunflower oil, plus more if desired
- Salt to taste

Directions:

1. Using the Bottom Blades in the Pitcher, add all of the ingredients and PULSE 5 times.
2. Select Speed 3 and flip the switch to START. Slowly increase to Speed 8 and blend until smooth, scraping down the sides as necessary. If desired, add oil until the butter is formed to your preference.
3. Refrigerate for up to 1 month

Frozen White Siberian

Servings:4 (7-ounce)
Cooking Time:x

Ingredients:

- 4 ounces coffee liqueur, plus additional for garnish
- 3 ounces vodka
- 1/2 cup lowfat milk
- 1 cup nonfat coffee frozen yogurt or ice cream
- 1 cup ice
- Whipped cream, for garnish

Directions:

1. Place all ingredients into the 72-ounce Pitcher in the order listed.
2. Press Auto-iQ BLEND.
3. Go ahead, embrace your inner meal prepper. We hear you, making smoothies the night before is a huge time saver. But, heads up, never store your smoothies with the blade assembly attached—active ingredients in some foods may lead to pressure buildup and possible injury. Store them with Sip & Seal Lids instead.

Thai Chicken Coconut Curry Soup

Servings:x
Cooking Time:x

Ingredients:

- 3 cups coconut milk, filtered, from a carton
- 2 tablespoons vegetable oil
- 3 cloves garlic, peeled
- 1 white onion, diced
- 3 cups chicken broth
- 3 tablespoons red curry paste
- 3 tablespoons soy sauce
- 3 tablespoons lime juice
- 1 tablespoon brown sugar
- 1 tablespoon ground turmeric
- 2 boneless chicken breasts, cut into 2-inch strips
- 4 cups rice stick noodles or vermicelli, cooked
- 1 cup bean sprouts
- lime wedges, for garnish
- cilantro leaves, chopped

Directions:

1. Heat oil in a stockpot and saute garlic and onion on medium heat until softened, about 10 minutes. Cool to room temperature.
2. Using the Bottom Blades in the Pitcher, add the cooled vegetables, coconut milk, chicken broth, curry paste, soy sauce, lime juice, brown sugar and turmeric. Select Speed 1 and flip the switch to START. Slowly increase to Speed 6 and blend until smooth.
3. Return mixture to the stockpot, add chicken and bring to a boil. Reduce heat and simmer for about 10 minutes, or until chicken is cooked through with no pink.

Crab Bisque

Servings:4-6
Cooking Time:20 Minutes

Ingredients:

- 1 tablespoon olive oil,
- 1 tablespoon butter,
- 1 carrot, peeled and chopped,
- 1 stalk celery, trimmed and chopped,
- 1/4 white onion, peeled and chopped,
- 1 potato, peeled and chopped,
- 5 cups fish stock,
- 1/4 cup brandy,
- 2 tablespoons tomato paste,
- 1 tablespoon Old Bay seasoning,
- 1/4 teaspoon cayenne pepper,
- 1/8 teaspoon ground allspice,
- 10 ounces lump crab meat,
- 1 cup evaporated milk

Directions:

1. Set Ninja Cooking System to STOVETOP HIGH and add oil and butter to pot. Add carrot, celery, onion and potato. Sauté until just softened.
2. Add fish stock, brandy, tomato paste and seasonings. Bring to a boil.
3. Reduce heat, add half of the crab meat and gently simmer for 10 minutes. Cool to room temperature.
4. Using the Bottom Blades in the Pitcher of the ULTIMA blender, add the soup in batches.
5. Select Speed 1 and flip the switch to START. Slowly increase to Speed 6 and blend for 30 seconds or until smooth.*
6. Return soup to the Ninja Cooking System, set to STOVETOP MED and stir in evaporated milk, remaining crab meat and simmer until thoroughly heated through, about 15 minutes. Serve hot in bowls.

Tropical Chill

Servings:2-4
Cooking Time:x

Ingredients:

- 1 banana,
- 1/2 cup pineapple,
- 1/2 cup honeydew melon,
- 1/4 lime,
- 3/4 cup coconut water,
- 1 cup ice

Directions:

1. Place the Top Blades in the Pitcher and add all of the ingredients in the order listed.*
2. PULSE 3 times. Select Speed 10 and flip the switch to START. Blend for 45 seconds.

Classic Hummus

Servings:2 Cups
Cooking Time:x

Ingredients:
- 1 can (14 ounces) garbanzo beans, drained, liquid reserved
- 1/4 cup plus 2 tablespoons garbanzo bean liquid
- 1 garlic clove
- 2 tablespoons fresh lemon juice
- 2 tablespoons olive oil
- 1 tablespoon tahini
- 1/2 teaspoon ground cumin
- 1/2 teaspoon salt
- Cut vegetables and pita chips, for dipping

Directions:
1. Place all ingredients into the 24-ounce Tritan Nutri Ninja in the order listed.
2. Select START/STOP and blend until smooth. Remove the blades from the cup after blending. Transfer mixture to a serving bowl. Serve with cut vegetables and pita chips.
3. Go ahead, embrace your inner meal prepper. We hear you, making smoothies the night before is a huge time saver. But, heads up, never store your smoothies with the blade assembly attached—active ingredients in some foods may lead to pressure buildup and possible injury. Store them with Sip & Seal Lids instead.

Blender Mole Sauce

Servings:makes About 2 1/2 Cups.
Cooking Time:30 Minutes

Ingredients:

- 1 14-ounce can tomatoes,
- 1 chipotle chile, or more according to taste,
- 3/4 cup chicken broth,
- 1/4 cup almond butter,
- 1/2 onion, peeled and quartered,
- 2 cloves garlic, peeled,
- 3 tablespoons raisins,
- 2 tablespoons unsweetened cocoa powder,
- 1 tablespoon New Mexican ground red chile powder,
- 1 teaspoon ground cumin,
- 1/2 teaspoon ground cinnamon,
- 1/2 teaspoon ground cloves,
- 1 teaspoon brown sugar,
- salt to taste

Directions:

1. Place the Top Blades in the Pitcher and add all of the ingredients in the order listed.
2. Select Speed 3 and flip the switch to START. Slowly increase to Speed 6 and process until smooth.
3. Transfer to a saucepan and simmer, stirring occasionally until slightly reduced, about 20 minutes.

Kiwi-c Boost

Servings:1 12-ounce Serving
Cooking Time:x

Ingredients:
- 1 kiwi, peeled
- 1/4 avocado
- 1/2 lime, juiced
- 1/2 cup frozen pineapple
- 1 cup unsweetened coconut milk (in carton)
- 1 teaspoon agave

Directions:
1. Place all ingredients into the Ninja Ultima Single Serve in the order listed. PULSE until smooth. Remove the blades from the cup after blending.
2. Go ahead, embrace your inner meal prepper. We hear you, making smoothies the night before is a huge time saver. But, heads up, never store your smoothies with the blade assembly attached—active ingredients in some foods may lead to pressure buildup and possible injury. Store them with Sip & Seal Lids instead.

Sweet Potato And Carrot Latkes

Servings:4-6
Cooking Time:15 Minutes

Ingredients:

- 1 pound sweet potatoes, peeled and cut into 1" pieces,
- 1/2 pound carrots, peeled and cut into 1" pieces,
- 1/2 small onion, cut in quarters,
- clove garlic,
- 1/3 cup all-purpose flour,
- 2 large eggs, lightly beaten,
- 1/2 teaspoon salt,
- 1/4 teaspoon pepper,
- 3/4 cup vegetable oil

Directions:

1. Place the Top Blades in the Ninja Ultima Pitcher and add sweet potato and carrots. PULSE 3–5 times until evenly finely chopped. Remove to a bowl and rinse out Pitcher.
2. Place onion and garlic pieces in the Pitcher. PULSE until the onion and garlic are finely chopped. Add to sweet potatoes and carrots.
3. Add flour, eggs, salt and pepper to the sweet potato mixture and gently combine, being sure not to over mix.
4. Set Ninja Cooking System to STOVETOP HIGH. Add 2 tablespoons oil to pot. Spoon 1/8 cup sweet potato mixture into oil and flatten to 3–inch diameter with spatula. Cook until golden brown, about 1 1/2 minutes on each side. Place cooked latkes on paper towels to drain. Adding more oil as necessary, continue to cook sweet potato mixture. Serve with chilled Apple Pear Sauce.

Green Slime Smoothie

Servings:4
Cooking Time:x

Ingredients:

- 1 cup frozen pineapple
- 1 cup frozen peaches
- 1 small banana
- 1 cup spinach
- 1/2 cup water
- 1 cup ice

Directions:

1. Place the Top Blades in the Ninja Ultima Pitcher. Add coconut, yogurt, pineapple, almond milk and ice to the Pitcher.
2. PULSE 3 times. Select Speed 8 and flip the switch to START. Blend for 45 seconds or until smooth.*

Pomegranate Blue Smoothie

Servings:x
Cooking Time:x

Ingredients:

- 15 ounces frozen blueberries
- 2 1/4 cups pomegranate juice
- 4 1/2 ounces light silken tofu

Directions:

1. Place all ingredients in the order listed into a Ninja 72-ounce Pitcher and blend on High Speed for 45 seconds or until smooth.
2. Go ahead, embrace your inner meal prepper. We hear you, making smoothies the night before is a huge time saver. But, heads up, never store your smoothies with the blade assembly attached—active ingredients in some foods may lead to pressure buildup and possible injury. Store them with Sip & Seal Lids instead.

Cool Honeydew Cleanser

Servings:1-2
Cooking Time:x

Ingredients:

- 1/2 honeydew melon, peeled,
- 1/2 pineapple, peeled and chunked,
- 1 cucumber, peeled and quartered,
- 3/4 cup water,
- 1 cup ice cubes

Directions:

1. Place the Top Blades in the Pitcher and add all of the ingredients in the order listed.
2. Select Speed 1 and flip the switch to START. Slowly increase to Speed 6 and blend until smooth.

Island Mood Boost

Servings:4
Cooking Time:x

Ingredients:

- 2 cups coconut water,
- 1 cup pineapple, cut into 1-inch cubes,
- 1 cup frozen mango,
- 1 cup frozen strawberries,
- 1 banana,
- 2 teaspoons flaxseed

Directions:

1. Place the Top Blades in the Pitcher and add all of the ingredients in the order listed.*
2. PULSE 3 times. Select Speed 10 and flip the switch to START. Blend for 45 seconds.
3. Go ahead, embrace your inner meal prepper. We hear you, making smoothies the night before is a huge time saver. But, heads up, never store your smoothies with the blade assembly attached—active ingredients in some foods may lead to pressure buildup and possible injury. Store them with Sip & Seal Lids instead.

White Bean And Chicken Chili

Servings:6-8
Cooking Time:60 Minutes

Ingredients:

- 2 tablespoons olive oil,
- 1 onion, peeled and chopped,
- 1 green bell pepper, cored and chopped,
- 3 cloves garlic, peeled and smashed,
- 3/4 pound boneless, skinless chicken breasts, well-chilled,
- salt and pepper to taste,
- 1 tablespoon ground cumin,
- 2 teaspoons dried oregano,
- 1 teaspoon ground red chile pepper,
- 3 cans cannellini beans, 2 cans drained,
- 2 4-ounce cans diced green chiles,
- 3 cups chicken broth,
- 1/2 cup white cheddar cheese, shredded, as garnish,
- 2 tablespoons fresh cilantro leaves, chopped, as garnish

Directions:

1. In a large stockpot over medium heat, heat the oil and add the onion, bell pepper and garlic. Sauté and stir until softened.
2. Place the Top Blades in the Pitcher and add chicken. PULSE to a fine chop. Do not overprocess.
3. Add the chicken to the stockpot, along with the salt, pepper, cumin, oregano and chile. Stir in 2 cans drained beans, green chiles and chicken broth.
4. Place remaining can of beans with liquid in the Pitcher and PULSE until smooth. Add to chili and simmer for 30 to 40 minutes until slightly thickened.
5. Garnish each serving with cheese and cilantro.
6. Go ahead, embrace your inner meal prepper. We hear you, making smoothies the night before is a huge time saver. But, heads up, never store your smoothies with the blade assembly attached—active ingredients in some foods may lead to pressure buildup and possible injury. Store them with Sip & Seal Lids instead.

Lucky Green Smoothie

Servings:2 8-ounce
Cooking Time:x

Ingredients:

- 1 kiwi
- 1 cup spinach
- 3/4 cup coconut water
- 1 teaspoon agave
- 1/2 lime, peeled
- 3 to 4 ice cubes

Directions:

1. Add all ingredients in the order listed into the Single Serve and process until smooth. Remove the blades from the cup after blending.
2. Go ahead, embrace your inner meal prepper. We hear you, making smoothies the night before is a huge time saver. But, heads up, never store your smoothies with the blade assembly attached—active ingredients in some foods may lead to pressure buildup and possible injury. Store them with Sip Seal Lids instead.

Melon Basil Purifier

Servings:2-4
Cooking Time:x

Ingredients:

- 2 cups honeydew melon,
- 1/2 medium cucumber, cut lengthwise,
- 1/4 lime, peel removed,
- 1 cup kale,
- 4 to 5 basil leaves,
- 1 cup ice

Directions:

1. Place the Top Blades in the Pitcher and add all of the ingredients in the order listed.*
2. PULSE 3 times. Select Speed 10 and flip the switch to START. Blend for 45 seconds.

Blender Eggnog

Servings:6-8
Cooking Time:x

Ingredients:

- 6 eggs,
- 3/4 cup sugar,
- 1 teaspoon freshly grated nutmeg, plus additional for garnish,
- 3/4 cup brandy,
- 1/2 cup spiced or dark rum,
- 3 1/2 cups low-fat milk,
- 1/2 cup heavy cream

Directions:

1. Using the Bottom Blades in the Ninja Ultima Pitcher, add the eggs and sugar.
2. Select Speed 1 and flip the switch to START. Slowly increase to Speed 6 and blend for 10 seconds. Add all of the remaining ingredients and blend for 30 seconds.*
3. Chill completely before serving. Garnish with a sprinkle of freshly grated nutmeg.

Artichoke Hummus

Servings:6-8
Cooking Time:x

Ingredients:

- 2 15-ounce cans chickpeas, drained,
- 2 14-ounce cans artichoke hearts, drained,
- 1/2 cup lemon juice,
- 4 tablespoons roasted garlic,
- 1/4 cup parsley,
- Salt and fresh pepper to taste

Directions:

1. Place the Top Blades in the Ninja Ultima Pitcher, and add all of the ingredients in the order listed.
2. PULSE 3 times.
3. Select Speed 3 and flip the switch to START. Slowly increase to Speed 8 and blend for 45 seconds or until smooth. Add a little water if needed.*
4. Serve chilled or at room temperature.

Sunshine Pick-me-up

Servings:1
Cooking Time:x

Ingredients:

- 1 banana,
- 1 cup fresh or canned pineapple,
- 1/2 small cucumber, peeled, cut in half,
- 3/4 cup coconut water,
- 1/2 lime, juiced,
- 1 scoop vanilla protein powder,
- 3 to 4 ice cubes

Directions:

1. Place all of the ingredients into the Nutri Ninja cup in the order listed. PULSE until smooth. Remove the blades from the cup after blending.
2. Go ahead, embrace your inner meal prepper. We hear you, making smoothies the night before is a huge time saver. But, heads up, never store your smoothies with the blade assembly attached—active ingredients in some foods may lead to pressure buildup and possible injury. Store them with Sip & Seal Lids instead.

Sriracha

Servings:x
Cooking Time:x

Ingredients:

- 1 pound fresno or red jalapeno peppers, seeded and roughly chopped
- 6 cloves garlic
- 1/4 cup brown sugar
- 1 1/2 teaspoon kosher salt
- 1/3 cup distilled white vinegar

Directions:

1. Heat all of the ingredients in a medium saucepan.
2. Bring to a boil, and reduce to a simmer for 5 to 7 minutes. Allow to cool to room temperature.
3. Place the Top Blades in the Pitcher and add all of the ingredients.
4. Select Speed 1 and flip the switch to START. Slowly increase to Speed 8 and blend until smooth.
5. Store in the refrigerator in an airtight container.

Top O' The Day Immunity

Servings:1 12-ounce
Cooking Time:x

Ingredients:

- 1/2 banana
- 1/2 teaspoon fresh ginger root
- 1/2 teaspoon turmeric
- 3/4 cup coconut milk (in carton)
- 2 tablespoons lime juice
- 1 cup spinach
- 1 teaspoon agave
- 4-5 ice cubes

Directions:

1. Add all ingredients in order listed into the Single Serve and process until smooth. Remove the blades from the cup after blending.

2. Go ahead, embrace your inner meal prepper. We hear you, making smoothies the night before is a huge time saver. But, heads up, never store your smoothies with the blade assembly attached—active ingredients in some foods may lead to pressure buildup and possible injury. Store them with Sip & Seal Lids instead.

Asparagus And Watercress Soup With White Beans

Servings:4

Cooking Time:30 Minutes

Ingredients:

- 1 1/2 pounds asparagus 1 shallot, peeled, chopped
- 1 garlic clove, peeled, chopped
- 4 cups vegetable or chicken stock
- 1 15-ounce can white cannellini beans, rinsed and drained
- 1 cup watercress
- 2 tablespoons unsalted butter
- 1 tablespoon extra-virgin olive oil
- 1/4 teaspoon freshly ground black pepper
- 1 teaspoon salt
- Gremolata to garnish

Directions:

1. Trim tips from the asparagus, about 1 to 1 1/2 inches in length and set aside. Cut the stem end from each spear, about 1/2 inches in length and discard. Cut the remaining tender stalks into 1/2-inch pieces.
2. Place butter and 1 tablespoon olive oil into the pot. Set to STOVETOP HIGH and heat until butter is melted. Add the shallots and garlic and cook until fragrant, about 1 minute. Add the chopped asparagus stalks, salt and pepper, and cook, stirring, for 2 minutes. Add the vegetable stock and beans, simmer for 15 minutes. Add the asparagus tips and watercress and continue cooking for 5 more minutes until the asparagus is tender. Remove from the heat. Cool to room temperature.
3. Place Bottom Blades in the 72-ounce Pitcher. Add soup to the Pitcher and select Speed 1. Flip the switch to START and slowly increase to Speed 6, blending until smooth.
4. Place soup back in the pot and cook until heated through. Garnish with gremolata.

Raspberry Mango

Servings:1
Cooking Time:x

Ingredients:

- 1/2 cup fresh mango, peeled and pitted,
- 1 cup raspberries,
- 1/2 lemon, juiced,
- 1/2 cup apple juice,
- 4 ice cubes

Directions:

1. Place all of the ingredients into the Nutri Ninja cup in the order listed. PULSE until smooth. Remove the blades from the cup after blending.
2. Go ahead, embrace your inner meal prepper. We hear you, making smoothies the night before is a huge time saver. But, heads up, never store your smoothies with the blade assembly attached—active ingredients in some foods may lead to pressure buildup and possible injury. Store them with Sip & Seal Lids instead.

Mother Earth Cranberry Oaties

Servings:6-8
Cooking Time:25 Minutes

Ingredients:

- 1/2 cup coconut oil
- 1 egg
- 1/2 teaspoon vanilla extract
- 1/2 cup packed brown sugar
- 1/2 cup granulated sugar
- 1 1/4 cups King Arthur gluten-free flour blend
- 1/2 cup almond meal
- 1/2 cup gluten free oats
- 1/4 cup coconut, shredded, unsweetened
- 1/4 teaspoon baking soda
- 1 teaspoon kosher salt
- 1/2 teaspoon ground cinnamon
- 1/2 cup dried cranberries

Directions:

1. Preheat oven to 350F.
2. Using the Ninja Food Processor dough blade, add the coconut oil, egg, vanilla, brown sugar and granulated sugar to the food processor bowl. PULSE 3 times then blend for 15 seconds on MEDIUM to "cream" together the ingredients. Scrape down the sides.
3. In a medium bowl combine the flour, almond meal, oats, coconut, baking soda, salt and cinnamon and stir to combine. Add half of the dry mixture to the food processor bowl. PULSE 3 times then blend for 10 seconds on MEDIUM. Scrape down sides then add remaining dry mixture. Continue to blend another 15 seconds on MEDIUM until dough is evenly combined.
4. Add the cranberries to the food processor bowl and PULSE 10 times, until cranberries are evenly dispersed throughout dough.
5. Spoon tablespoon sized cookie dough onto parchment-lined cookie sheets, about 2 inches apart. Bake 10-12 minutes until JUST golden. Cookies will be very soft upon oven removal but will set up within 5 minutes of resting.

Peanut Butter Protein Pizzazz

Servings:2-4
Cooking Time:x

Ingredients:

- 1 scoop chocolate protein powder,
- 2 teaspoons unsweetened cocoa powder,
- 2 tablespoons creamy, unsalted, peanut butter,
- 3/4 cup almond milk,
- 1 cup ice

Directions:

1. Add all of the ingredients to the Nutri Ninja cup in the order listed. PULSE until creamy. Remove the blades from the cup after blending.
2. Go ahead, embrace your inner meal prepper. We hear you, making smoothies the night before is a huge time saver. But, heads up, never store your smoothies with the blade assembly attached—active ingredients in some foods may lead to pressure buildup and possible injury. Store them with Sip Seal Lids instead.

Butternut Squash Blast

Servings:3-4
Cooking Time:x

Ingredients:

- 2 1/4 cups butternut or acorn squash, seeded, peeled and oven-roasted
- 2 1/4 cups almond milk, unsweetened
- 1/3 cup walnuts, shelled
- 1 1/2 tablespoons real maple syrup
- 3 teaspoons ground turmeric
- 1 1/2 teaspoons cinnamon
- 3/4 cup ice

Directions:

1. Place all the ingredients in the order listed into a Ninja 72-ounce Pitcher and blend on High Speed for 45 seconds or until smooth.

Watermelon Quench

Servings:4 (8-ounce)
Cooking Time:x

Ingredients:

- 2 1/2 cups fresh watermelon chunks
- 2 cups pomegranate juice
- 1 cup frozen peaches

Directions:

1. Place all ingredients into the 72-ounce Pitcher in the order listed.
2. Press Auto-iQ BLEND.
3. Go ahead, embrace your inner meal prepper. We hear you, making smoothies the night before is a huge time saver. But, heads up, never store your smoothies with the blade assembly attached—active ingredients in some foods may lead to pressure buildup and possible injury. Store them with Sip & Seal Lids instead.

3-2-1 Immune Boost

Servings:1-2
Cooking Time:x

Ingredients:

- 3 tangerines, peeled,
- 2 kiwis, peeled and halved,
- 1 grapefruit, peeled and halved,
- 1 tablespoon dried goji berries,
- 1 cup water,
- 1 cup ice cubes

Directions:

1. Place the Top Blades in the Pitcher and add all of the ingredients in the order listed.*
2. Select Speed 1 and flip the switch to START. Slowly increase to Speed 8 and blend until smooth.

Pineapple Lime Popsicles

Servings:6
Cooking Time:x

Ingredients:

- 2 cups pineapple chunks,
- 3 tablespoons lime juice,
- 1/4 teaspoon red chile powder

Directions:

1. Using the Bottom Blades in the Pitcher, add all of the ingredients and PULSE 5 times, scraping the sides as necessary.
2. Select Speed 3 and flip the switch to START. Slowly increase to Speed 6 and process until smooth.
3. Pour into popsicle molds and freeze until solid.

Ground Chicken Lettuce Boats

Servings:4-6
Cooking Time:20 Minutes

Ingredients:
- 2 boneless, skinless chicken breasts, well-chilled,
- 2 teaspoons canola oil, divided,
- 1 red bell pepper, seeded and chopped,
- 1 8-ounce can water chestnuts, sliced,
- 4 green onions, finely chopped,
- 4 leaves napa cabbage, chopped,
- 1 1-inch piece ginger, peeled and minced,
- 1/4 cup Asian stir-fry sauce, divided,
- 1/4 bunch cilantro leaves, chopped,
- 6 to 10 romaine lettuce or napa cabbage leaves,
- 1/4 cup peanuts, chopped,
- 1 lime, cut in wedges

Directions:
1. Place the Top Blades in the Pitcher and add chicken breasts. PULSE chicken to a fine chop. Do not overprocess.
2. Heat 1 teaspoon oil over medium-high heat in a large sauté pan and stir-fry bell pepper, water chestnuts, onions, cabbage and ginger until just softened, about 2 to 5 minutes. Set aside.
3. Heat remaining oil in sauté pan, add chicken and stir-fry until no longer pink, about 4 to 5 minutes.
4. Add 2 tablespoons Asian stir-fry sauce and toss with chicken to coat. Stir in cilantro, and reserved vegetable mixture and add remaining sauce and cook until vegetables are heated.
5. Serve in lettuce leaves garnished with chopped peanuts. Pass lime wedges.

Bright Side Banana Mocha Shake

Servings:2-4
Cooking Time:x

Ingredients:

- 1 banana,
- 1/2 cup brewed coffee, chilled,
- 3 tablespoons creamy almond butter,
- 2 teaspoons unsweetened cocoa powder,
- 1 teaspoon agave nectar,
- 1 cup almond milk,
- 2 cups ice

Directions:

1. Place the Top Blades in the Pitcher and add all of the ingredients in the order listed.*
2. PULSE 3 times. Select Speed 10 and flip the switch to START. Blend for 45 seconds.
3. Go ahead, embrace your inner meal prepper. We hear you, making smoothies the night before is a huge time saver. But, heads up, never store your smoothies with the blade assembly attached—active ingredients in some foods may lead to pressure buildup and possible injury. Store them with Sip & Seal Lids instead.

Strawberry Melon Energy Blast

Servings:2-4
Cooking Time:x

Ingredients:

- 2 cups cantaloupe,
- 1/2 medium cucumber, peeled, cut lengthwise,
- 8 strawberries, stems removed,
- 1 cup ice

Directions:

1. Place the Top Blades in the Pitcher and add all of the ingredients in the order listed.*
2. PULSE 3 times. Select Speed 10 and flip the switch to START. Blend for 45 seconds.
3. Go ahead, embrace your inner meal prepper. We hear you, making smoothies the night before is a huge time saver. But, heads up, never store your smoothies with the blade assembly attached—active ingredients in some foods may lead to pressure buildup and possible injury. Store them with Sip & Seal Lids instead.

Green Chicken Curry

Servings:x
Cooking Time:x

Ingredients:
- Marinade:
- 1/2 cup reduced-sodium soy sauce or low sodium Liquid Aminos
- 1 orange, juiced
- 2 tablespoons honey
- 2 tablespoons canola oil
- 1-1 1/2 pounds chicken, boneless, skinless thighs or breasts
- 2 tablespoons canola oil, divided
- 1 garlic clove, chopped
- 1/4 cup green Thai curry paste
- 1 14-ounce can unsweetened coconut milk
- 1/4 cup fresh cilantro and/or mint
- 1 tablespoon fresh lime juice
- 1 teaspoon agave
- 1 red pepper, cored and cut into 1-inch chunks
- 1 green pepper, cored and cut into 1-inch chunks
- 1 small red onion, peeled and cut into 1-inch chunks
- Kosher salt and freshly ground pepper

Directions:
1. Combine marinade ingredients in a bowl. Add chicken and marinate for 1 to 2 hours. Drain chicken from marinade and discard.
2. To make the green curry sauce, add 1 tablespoon canola oil, garlic, green Thai curry paste, coconut milk, cilantro and mint, lime juice and agave to the food processor bowl fitted with the steel quad blade. Process until smooth.
3. Set the Cooking System to STOVETOP HIGH. Add remaining 1 tablespoon of oil and add red pepper, green pepper and onion and sauté, stirring occasionally until slightly softened; remove vegetables and set aside. Add chicken and sear meat on all sides. Add green curry sauce and simmer chicken until cooked through and sauce thickens, stirring occasionally. Add vegetables back into pot to reheat. Season with salt and pepper to taste.
4. Serve over brown or white rice.

Almond Milk

Servings:x
Cooking Time:x

Ingredients:
- 1 cup raw almonds
- 3 cups water

Directions:
1. Place the Top Blades in the Pitcher and add all of the ingredients in the order listed (use less water if a thicker milk is desired). Select Speed 1 and flip the switch to START. Slowly increase to Speed 8 and blend for 60 seconds.
2. Pour mixture through a filtration bag or a fine mesh strainer to extract milk. Store in refrigerator for up to 3 days.

Strawberry Daiquiri

Servings:2
Cooking Time:x

Ingredients:

- 1/2 cup strawberries, hulled, plus 2 whole for garnish,
- 2 ounces lime juice,
- 4 ounces light rum,
- 1 cup ice cubes

Directions:

1. Place all of the ingredients into the Single Serve Cup in the order listed. PULSE until smooth. Remove the blades from the cup after blending. Garnish each serving with a whole strawberry.
2. Go ahead, embrace your inner meal prepper. We hear you, making smoothies the night before is a huge time saver. But, heads up, never store your smoothies with the blade assembly attached—active ingredients in some foods may lead to pressure buildup and possible injury. Store them with Sip & Seal Lids instead.

Butternut Squash Soup

Servings:6 (8-ounce)
Cooking Time:35–40 Minutes

Ingredients:

- 3 tablespoons olive oil
- 1 large yellow onion, chopped
- 1 cup raw cashews
- 1 large apple, peeled, cored, chopped
- 1 large carrot, peeled, chopped
- 2 pounds butternut squash, peeled, cubed
- 1 teaspoon fresh thyme leaves
- 1 bay leaf
- 4 cups vegetable broth
- 1/2 teaspoon salt
- Ground black pepper, to taste

Directions:

1. Heat oil in a large saucepan and add onions, cooking until they begin to soften, about 5 minutes. Add cashews and cook, stirring, about 5 minutes.
2. Add apple, carrot, squash, thyme leaves, and bay leaf to pot and cook for 5 minutes. Add broth and stir to combine. Bring soup to a boil and reduce heat to medium-low, simmering until squash is easily pierced with a knife, 20 to 25 minutes. Remove from heat; remove and discard bay leaf.
3. Allow soup to cool to room temperature. Ladle cooled soup into the 72-ounce Pitcher. Select HIGH and blend until smooth, about 1 minute. Return soup to saucepan and simmer until heated through. Add salt and pepper to taste.
4. Go ahead, embrace your inner meal prepper. We hear you, making smoothies the night before is a huge time saver. But, heads up, never store your smoothies with the blade assembly attached—active ingredients in some foods may lead to pressure buildup and possible injury. Store them with Sip & Seal Lids instead.

Calm-ond Milk

Servings:makes 3 Cups
Cooking Time:x

Ingredients:

- 1 cup raw almonds,
- 3 cups water

Directions:

1. Place the Top Blades in the Pitcher and add all of the ingredients in the order listed (use less water if a thicker milk is desired).*
2. Select Speed 1 and flip the switch to START. Slowly increase to Speed 8 and blend for 60 seconds.
3. Pour mixture through a filtration bag or a fine mesh strainer to extract milk.
4. Store in refrigerator for up to 3 days.

Top O' The Mornin' Smoothie

Servings:1
Cooking Time:x

Ingredients:

- 1 banana, peeled,
- 1 orange, peeled, cut in half,
- 1/2 teaspoon ground cinnamon,
- 1 scoop protein powder,
- 1 cup vanilla almond milk,
- 5 to 6 ice cubes

Directions:

1. Place all of the ingredients into the Nutri Ninja cup in the order listed. PULSE until smooth. Remove the blades from the cup after blending.
2. Go ahead, embrace your inner meal prepper. We hear you, making smoothies the night before is a huge time saver. But, heads up, never store your smoothies with the blade assembly attached—active ingredients in some foods may lead to pressure buildup and possible injury. Store them with Sip & Seal Lids instead.

Berry Healthy Smoothie

Servings:2-3
Cooking Time:x

Ingredients:

- 1 cup blueberries,
- 1 cup strawberries, hulled,
- 2 mangoes, peeled and pitted,
- 1 cup pineapple chunks,
- 1 cup baby spinach,
- 1 cup water,
- 1 cup ice cubes

Directions:

1. Place the Top Blades in the Pitcher and add all of the ingredients in the order listed.*
2. Select Speed 1 and flip the switch to START. Slowly increase to Speed 8 and blend until smooth.
3. Go ahead, embrace your inner meal prepper. We hear you, making smoothies the night before is a huge time saver. But, heads up, never store your smoothies with the blade assembly attached—active ingredients in some foods may lead to pressure buildup and possible injury. Store them with Sip & Seal Lids instead.

Carrot Ginger Soup

Servings:x
Cooking Time:x

Ingredients:

- 2 tablespoons olive oil
- 6 medium carrots, peeled and chopped
- 4 shallots, peeled and chopped
- 1 2-inch piece fresh turmeric root, peeled and chopped (about the size of your little finger)
- 1 1 1/2-inch piece fresh ginger root, peeled and chopped (about the size of your thumb)
- 1 1/2 cups vegetable broth
- 2 tablespoons fresh lime juice salt and pepper to taste

Directions:

1. Heat oil in a stockpot over medium-high heat and sauté carrots, shallot, turmeric and ginger until softened, about 15 minutes.
2. Add vegetable broth, lime juice, salt and pepper and simmer for 10 to 15 minutes on medium-low heat. Cool to room temperature.
3. Using the Bottom Blades in the Pitcher, add the soup. Select Speed 1 and flip the switch to START. Slowly increase to Speed 6 and blend until smooth.
4. Reheat soup in the stockpot until hot throughout or chill in the refrigerator before serving.

Super Ninja 9

Servings:4
Cooking Time:x

Ingredients:

- 2 tomatoes, quartered,
- 1 cucumber, peeled and quartered,
- 1 stalk celery, cut into thirds,
- 1 Granny Smith apple, quartered, unpeeled and uncored,
- 1 small carrot, peeled and cut in half,
- 1-inch piece of red onion,
- 1/2 jalapeno pepper, seeded,
- 1/4 beet, peeled,
- 1/2 cup red cabbage, shredded,
- 1 1/2 cups ice,
- 1/2 teaspoon sea salt

Directions:

1. Place the Top Blades in the Pitcher and add all of the ingredients in the order listed.*
2. PULSE 3 times. Select Speed 10 and flip the switch to START. Blend for 45 seconds.

Autumn Balancer

Servings:2-4
Cooking Time:x

Ingredients:

- 5 ounces steamed sweet potato,
- 1 cup almond or coconut milk,
- 2 tablespoons maple syrup,
- 1 teaspoon flaxseeds,
- 1/4 teaspoon ground turmeric,
- 1 1/2 cups ice cubes

Directions:

1. Place the Top Blades in the Pitcher and add all of the ingredients in the order listed.*
2. PULSE 3 times. Select Speed 10 and flip the switch to START. Blend for 45 seconds.
3. Go ahead, embrace your inner meal prepper. We hear you, making smoothies the night before is a huge time saver. But, heads up, never store your smoothies with the blade assembly attached—active ingredients in some foods may lead to pressure buildup and possible injury. Store them with Sip & Seal Lids instead.

Frozen Pina Colada

Servings:2
Cooking Time:x

Ingredients:

- 4 ounces light rum,
- 3/4 cup Coconut Milk,
- 1/2 cup pineapple chunks,
- 1 cup ice cubes

Directions:

1. Place all of the ingredients in the Single Serve Cup in the order listed. PULSE until smooth. Remove the blades from the cup after blending. Pour into tall decorative glasses and serve with a straw.
2. Go ahead, embrace your inner meal prepper. We hear you, making smoothies the night before is a huge time saver. But, heads up, never store your smoothies with the blade assembly attached—active ingredients in some foods may lead to pressure buildup and possible injury. Store them with Sip & Seal Lids instead.

Spring Pea Puree

Servings:4
Cooking Time:5 Minutes

Ingredients:

- 2 cups frozen peas, cooked and cooled
- 1/4 cup fresh mint leaves
- 1 garlic clove
- 1/2 teaspoon Kosher salt
- 1/2 teaspoon freshly ground black pepper
- 1/4 cup extra-virgin olive oil
- 1/4 cup vegetable broth
- 1/2 cup grated Parmesan cheese

Directions:

1. Combine all the ingredients in a food processor and puree. Transfer pea puree to a small bowl and stir in cheese.
2. Used in our recipe for Lemon Roasted Salmon with Spring Pea Puree.

Blackberry Mint Italian Ice

Servings:4

Cooking Time:25 Minutes + Chill Time: 6 Hours

Ingredients:

- 2 cups fresh blackberries,
- 1 cup water,
- 1 cup sugar,
- 1/4 cup fresh mint leaves

Directions:

1. Using the Bottom Blades in the Pitcher, add the blackberries and water and PULSE 2 times.
2. Select Speed 1 and flip the switch to START. Slowly increase to Speed 6 and process until smooth.
3. Strain through a fine mesh strainer into a saucepan.
4. Add sugar and mint and slowly bring to a boil to dissolve sugar.
5. Cool completely and strain into a 9 x 9-inch glass dish. Freeze for 6 hours, stirring frozen crystals every 30 minutes.
6. Serve or store in the freezer for up to 2 weeks.

Pumpkin Cheesecake With Gingersnap Pecan Crust

Servings:8-10
Cooking Time:55 Minutes

Ingredients:
- 1/2 cup raw pecans,
- 30 gingersnaps,
- 6 tablespoons unsalted butter, melted,
- 1/4 cup sugar,
- 1/4 teaspoon salt,
- 1/2 teaspoon vanilla,
- 16 ounces cream cheese,
- 1 cup sugar,
- 1/2 cup pumpkin, roasted and pureed or solid pack pumpkin,
- 2 teaspoon vanilla,
- 2 teaspoons pumpkin spice,
- 1/4 teaspoon salt,
- 3 large eggs

Directions:
1. Preheat oven to 350°F.
2. Place the Top Blades in the Ninja Ultima Pitcher and add pecans and gingersnaps; PULSE until flour-like consistency. Pour mixture into a medium bowl and add butter, sugar, salt and vanilla. Stir with fork until fully incorporated and press into bottom of an 8" springform pan, pressing crust 1" up the sides of pan.
3. Bake crust for 15 minutes, until puffed and set.
4. Place the Top Blades in the Ninja Ultima Pitcher and add the cream cheese, pumpkin, vanilla, salt and eggs. PULSE 8-10 times to combine the ingredients.
5. Select Speed 1 and flip the switch to START. Slowly increase to Speed 5 and blend for 15 seconds or until smooth.*
6. Set oven to 325°F, pour cheesecake filling into crust and bake for 40 minutes or until center is set.

Berries Galore

Servings:x
Cooking Time:x

Ingredients:

- 1 cup blackberries
- 1/2 cup raspberries
- 1/2 cup blueberries
- 2 small oranges, peeled and cut in half
- 1 cup ice

Directions:

1. Place the Top Blades in the Pitcher and add all of the ingredients in the order listed. Select Speed 1 and flip the switch to START. Slowly increase to Speed 8 and blend until smooth.
2. Go ahead, embrace your inner meal prepper. We hear you, making smoothies the night before is a huge time saver. But, heads up, never store your smoothies with the blade assembly attached—active ingredients in some foods may lead to pressure buildup and possible injury. Store them with Sip & Seal Lids instead.

Chocolate Banana Ice Cream

Servings:2-3
Cooking Time:x

Ingredients:

- 4 large frozen bananas, peeled and cut into 2-inch pieces,
- 1/2 cup chocolate syrup,
- 1/4 cup low-fat milk

Directions:

1. Place the Top Blades in the Pitcher and add all of the ingredients in the order listed. PULSE 5 times, scraping the sides as necessary.
2. Select Speed 3 and flip the switch to START. Slowly increase to Speed 6 and process until smooth.
3. Serve immediately or freeze.

Homemade Breakfast Bars

Servings:12
Cooking Time:x

Ingredients:

- 1 cup pecans, roasted
- 1 cup dried cranberries
- 1 cup dates, pitted
- 1 tablespoon chia seeds (optional)

Directions:

1. Place the Top Blades in the Pitcher and add all of the ingredients. PULSE to combine, scraping down sides as necessary.
2. Press into a plastic-lined 8 x 8-inch baking pan, cover and refrigerate for at least 1 hour.
3. Invert onto cutting board, remove plastic and cut into 12 bars. Wrap pieces in plastic wrap to store.

Super Green Smoothie

Servings:2-4
Cooking Time:x

Ingredients:
- 1/2 medium cucumber, peeled, and cut lengthwise,
- 1 cup honeydew melon,
- 12 green, seedless grapes,
- 1 large orange, peeled and halved,
- 1 cup spinach leaves,
- 1 cup ice

Directions:
1. Place the Top Blades in the Pitcher and add all of the ingredients in the order listed.*
2. PULSE 3 times. Select Speed 10 and flip the switch to START. Blend for 45 seconds.

Almond Honey Butter

Servings:makes 1 1/4 Cups
Cooking Time:x

Ingredients:
- 2 cups almonds, toasted,
- 1 tablespoon canola oil,
- 3 tablespoons honey,
- 1/8 teaspoon salt

Directions:
1. Place almonds in a single layer on a baking sheet and toast in a 375°F oven for 5 to 6 minutes. Cool and toss with oil.
2. Using the Bottom Blade in the Pitcher, add the almonds to the Pitcher. PULSE until finely chopped.
3. Add honey and salt and PULSE 5 times.
4. Select Speed 3 on the dial and flip the switch to START. Slowly increase to Speed 8 until smooth. Add more oil if desired.

Sweet Spinach Detox

Servings:1-2
Cooking Time:x

Ingredients:

- 2 crisp apples, peeled, cored, cut in half,
- 1 lemon, peeled,
- 1-inch ginger, peeled,
- 1 1/2 cups fresh spinach,
- 2 tablespoons agave or honey,
- 1/2 cup apple juice,
- 1/2 cup water,
- 1 cup ice cubes

Directions:

1. Place the Top Blades in the Pitcher and add all of the ingredients in the order listed.*
2. Select Speed 1 and flip the switch to START. Slowly increase to Speed 8 and blend until smooth.
3. Go ahead, embrace your inner meal prepper. We hear you, making smoothies the night before is a huge time saver. But, heads up, never store your smoothies with the blade assembly attached—active ingredients in some foods may lead to pressure buildup and possible injury. Store them with Sip & Seal Lids instead.

Apple Pie Smoothie

Servings:4 8-ounce
Cooking Time:x

Ingredients:

- 3 large golden delicious apples, peeled and cored,
- 1 teaspoon cinnamon,
- 2 pinches nutmeg,
- 2 pinches salt,
- 2 tablespoons brown sugar,
- 1 cup unsweetened almond milk,
- 2 cups ice

Directions:

1. Place the Top Blades in the Ninja Ultima Pitcher and add all of the ingredients in the order listed.
2. PULSE 3 times. Select Speed 10 and flip the switch to START. Blend for 45 seconds or until smooth. Taste and adjust spices as desired.
3. Garnish top of smoothies or glass rim with cookie or graham cracker crumbs.
4. Go ahead, embrace your inner meal prepper. We hear you, making smoothies the night before is a huge time saver. But, heads up, never store your smoothies with the blade assembly attached—active ingredients in some foods may lead to pressure buildup and possible injury. Store them with Sip & Seal Lids instead.

Chocolate Chile Frosty

Servings:4
Cooking Time:x

Ingredients:

- 1 cup low-fat chocolate milk,
- 3/4 cup tequila,
- 1 teaspoon vanilla extract,
- 1/2 teaspoon red chile powder,
- 1/2 teaspoon ground cinnamon,
- 2 cups nonfat chocolate frozen yogurt or ice cream,
- 1 cup ice cubes

Directions:

1. Place the Top Blades in the Pitcher and add all of the ingredients in the order listed.

2. Select Speed 1 and flip the switch to START. Slowly increase to Speed 8 and blend until smooth.

3. Serve in chilled margarita glasses.

Sweet Red Pepper Spread

Servings:6-8
Cooking Time:x

Ingredients:

- 1 15-ounce can garbanzo beans, drained,
- 1 4-ounce jar roasted red peppers, drained, reserving 1 tablespoon to thin, if desired,
- 1 tablespoon balsamic vinegar,
- 1/2 teaspoon Hungarian paprika,
- 1 tablespoon extra-virgin olive oil,
- 1/2 teaspoon kosher salt,
- 1/4 teaspoon black pepper

Directions:

1. Using the Bottom Blades in the Pitcher, add all of the ingredients in the order listed.
2. Select Speed 3 and flip the switch to START. Slowly increase to Speed 8 and process until smooth.
3. Scrape down the sides of the Pitcher as needed.
4. Serve the spread with toasted crostini or cracker rounds.

RECIPES INDEX

Printed in Great Britain
by Amazon

47934052R00066